The Eighth Gift

Richard J. Harding

The Christ Child Trilogy

Book 1

The Eighth Gift

ISBN: 978-0-578-45067-4

Cover and page design by Chelsea Jackson

Edited by Jackson Writing and Editing, LLC

Cover photo taken by Addison Marie Blacker

Praise for The Eighth Gift

"This is a breathtaking book. The writing is fabulous! This is a must-read book—especially at Christmas, Easter, Mother's Day, or any time someone wants to be moved and uplifted."

Katie C.

"A captivating experience!"

Dennis G.

"Richard Harding has a writing style and poetic license that is truly unique. It was like watching a movie."

Rick J.

"My wife passed away recently. I read your book seven times! It has changed my life! Thank you."

John R.

Acknowledgments

I want to express my appreciation to Addison Marie Blacker for her marvelous artwork. Special thanks goes to Chelsea Jackson for her insightful commentary and editing work. I especially appreciate the beautiful design work on the cover.

Contents

The Token

It was a winter of dissension; a tempest was raging. Of the strife which stresses mens' souls, this was a mighty struggle, a life-and-death struggle, or at least that was the issue at hand. A battle brought to bear because of the death of my friend . . . my friend, my companion and more . . . a son and daughter as well. They were the sweetness of my life; but sweetness, once gone, can leave a bitter taste.

Now the token in my hand was heavy to bear. We had matching tokens—emblems exchanged when life was sweet and young. They were symbols of that most valued in life. Now my friend and the other token were gone.

Mine offered no comfort. Instead it was unnerving,

disconcerting, a reminder of the pain, a burden to my heart.

Now the issues of life faded to one, and it was painfully clear: mortal life ends. Then what? Continuance or oblivion—that is the question, and the answer cannot have it both ways.

A coin has but two sides. Life is short. At the end is it heads or tails?

The Transformation

I live in a thriving city with towering buildings, noisy traffic, and bustling people everywhere—a most unsettling place to be sure. However, I have seen a transformation take place suddenly, almost overnight, as though a great invisible wand passed overhead, leaving a magical shower of crystal flakes behind. Flakes covered tall buildings, pine trees, parked cars—everything. Even fluffy gilded blankets adorned windowsills around town.

A new and exciting world met my eyes. An arcade of activities with carolers singing, Christmas chimes ringing, and the wonders of Santa filling the imagination of youthful hearts everywhere.

The air, too, was transformed. A fresh clean fragrance made me pause and slowly inhale great volumes of air and glow in the wonderment of being alive.

I examined the wonderland about me and marveled. Each year a rebirth takes place, a festive attitude takes hold, and a certain magic fills the air. Each year the wand passes over, leaving glowing embers in every heart it touches.

Suddenly, a switch turned on, a light ignited. My eyes sparkled, and I was happy to be alive. Alive, but . . . a lingering uneasiness, a questioning, demanding irritation, a persistent unreachable itch remained within.

The brilliantly shrouded cavern known as Main Street lured me into its sanctuary. A delightful escapade of colors, new scents, and aromas and fascinating lively window displays lined the street. The activities enveloped my senses . . . exciting them.

A certain mystique lingered in the air. A translucent cloud permeated the night. It was subtle, sometimes barely noticeable. Gentle in its touch, it whispered glowing, comforting, subliminal messages to my soul. I couldn't define its meaning, or if it had more than one meaning. It suggested this is more than a season, more than a holiday. It is something unique—something marvelous!

Still, there was that lingering uneasiness lurking within, unrelenting.

Up ahead I heard a bell, a constant double-beat calling my name. Responding to its call, I moved deeper into this enchanted world, leaving behind crisp precisely-defined footprints in the soft white carpet.

As my feet moved to the lazy clippety-clop serenade of horse-drawn buggies, I considered the meaning of it all. Such magic, and yet such oddity, such brazenness, such peculiar behavior— carolers singing to strangers, presents passed here and there, seasons greetings spread by one and all. I wondered, what force could affect such a transformation?

I found myself in a world filled with Christmas magic; yet, through it all, my friend was still gone.

I left to ponder the meaning of it. Not just the season, but everything. If this was more than a holiday, then what? Through it all, one mischievous mystery massaged my mind. If Christmas is a celebration of the beginning, what is the ending?

The Event

As I followed the sights and sounds, I was taken by the window displays. The first display to greet me hosted plump little snowmen in a skater's paradise. Another paraded numerous playful children who plundered a candy wonderland in obvious delight.

Highlighting the most festive display of all was a jolly soul wearing a sparkle in his eye and a laugh as lively as his belly. Contrasted against his beard, rosy red cheeks nearly glowed as bright as Rudolph's nose. His plump physique was round as a peach—a rather large peach!

It was the elves that caught my complete fascination. Laboring in their workshop, the elves were tiny little creatures that mystified me. It seemed the furious activity of their hammers kept cadence with the uneasiness within.

What a mysterious upheaval it was, an unrelenting disturbance exerting a mighty force, demanding a resolution, waiting, wanting to be unleashed. Like a thoroughbred, a Kentucky champion, high-spirited, energy-charged, anxious for his freedom, but trapped in the starting gate—constrained!

As I pondered the tempest within, soft, gentle notes descended into the night—a soothing ointment to my ears. Again the bell rang, resonating. I followed its beckoning.

It led me to the other display, more than a display—an event. It caught my eye, stopped me in mid-stride, and captured my soul.

The display wasn't outlandish. In fact, it was quiet in nature. It hosted humble shepherds, searching wise men, and a single majestic star—a pilgrim's star. It reached out to me saying, "Come see. I have hidden mysteries here awaiting your discovery."

It was the magnificence of the whole presentation that enthralled my imagination. It was inspiring, mysterious, a familiar voice, familiar and distant—but . . . what was it saying?

So involved in thought was I that I was unaware of the trip

home or of retiring to bed. Though kingly in size, my bed seemed a shrunken cage, and the soft sheets confined vines enfolding my thrashing limbs.

My mind was muddled, wondering, wandering, searching—for what?

Finally, a slumbering peace descended, but still I could hear the haunting words, "Come see . . . I have. . . ."

The Dream

Unlike most dreams, which are vague hazy phantoms that come and go, this was a clear, vivid drama that played itself before me. It was so astonishing that I still marvel at its occurrence.

There was a room, a large, spacious room with a seductive warmth that permeated every corner, reaching out, encouraging me to enter. I did so slowly, cautiously, with great curiosity. What took hold of my eyes stopped me instantly—it was breathtaking!

With an upward swivel of my head, I took in the room's dimensions. Filling the breadth of the room and looming before my view was the most elegant Christmas tree I had ever seen. I was astonished by its beauty and size. Towering in its proportions, it reached upward forever, ascending up and through the roof—

if indeed there was a roof.

Initially, I thought the pinnacle of the tree to be up and beyond my vision, but, in the subdued lighting, I could detect an object sitting upon its apex.

The tree was completely embellished in a soft, luminous cloud radiating from countless lights adorning the branches. In fact, the lights weren't lights at all, but millions of tiny little stars that shimmered and glowed. It was all I noticed, except, of course, the carefully wrapped presents.

Seven in number, they were huddled like children under the tree—children that uniquely differed in size and color . . . as though each had a message of its own. They had no customary bows; instead, tiny little ornaments—ornaments that hinted of contents hidden within—rested on each package.

The First Present

The first present to catch my interest was wrapped in deep blue like a dark, summer night—a fitting background for the tiny manger nestled in the corner. With a certain reverence, I took it in my hands. In the radiance of the countless stars overhead, I measured every detail. It had a soul of its own.

The effects stirred memories of a journey to ancient lands made not so long ago . . . and of a night spent in Bethlehem.

It was a night in the early spring when all things are fresh and new. It was a quiet, reflective night, night made for watching stars and pondering eternal mysteries. From a secluded refuge, I beheld a full, panoramic display of the distant horizon and all things in-between.

The Eight Gift

The plains and rolling hills were cradled in a brilliant, star-filled tapestry. In the stillness, a soothing spell secretly stretched out her hand and touched me. In quiet reflection, I could detect its presence. Strains of a distant melody lingered in the hills and quiet pastures. Something important had touched the land and left a timeless residue behind. A voice . . . a pleading voice called out to me. It drew me away into another night—a peaceful night, a quiet night, a most holy, silent night.

I could sense the unsuspecting shepherds enjoying the glowing embers of a dying fire as they had done a thousand nights before. But this night, a new light, a heavenly light, was to overshadow them and grace the earth. What sublime suspense was theirs to behold such a spectacle as, for one holy instant, the earth paused, the heavens opened, and they stood in wondering awe. What eyes have seen what they have seen, or ears have heard what theirs have heard . . . to marvel at heavenly choirs or to behold a child lying in a manger?

As I reflected upon that wondrous night when heavens filled with angels, I wondered, who were those heralding messengers from on high . . . and where was I?

Where was I during this epic time in history? Where was I

when the eternities paused, heaven and earth embraced, and the Holy One of Israel made His debut? Where was I when angels sang, and the hallelujah chorus filled the air? I wondered, where was I? And who were those angels, those heralding messengers, who entertained those few good shepherds that first early Christmas morn?

As I considered the stars and angels and choruses that filled the heavens, my eyes came back to the present cradled in my hands. It was then I realized the first gift was the gift of Christmas itself! And how well it should be, for what would Christmas be without the first Christmas?

The Ornament

As I placed the present back under the tree, my eyes traveled to a second package—a bright yellow package with a small figure of Christ. His outstretched arms each bore a young girl. One carried crutches; the other wore a resilient smile that seemed to have a secret message. She had my daughter's smile and the resemblance was striking. I found it curious that a ring, much like the one I still wore, should be upon her finger.

The ornament's beauty extended beyond its elegance. Realizing there was a deeper meaning, I looked more intently into its dimensions. As I did so, I was taken away as though in a trance.

I know not by what magic my mind traveled through the

ages or by what fortune I beheld the crowded streets. I only know the wonderment I felt as I experienced the sights, the sounds, and the smells.

I knew immediately I was in the ancient city, Jerusalem by name. With keen interest, I looked about. It was difficult not to be jostled to and fro by bustling people going here and there in different directions. It would take a man with a sturdy voice to be heard above the din and excitement.

The Carpenter

In spite of the distractions, it did not take long for me to find Him. I wouldn't say He was ordinary looking, but at first glance there was nothing unusual about Him to look upon. His clothing and facial features were fairly typical of His country, and He blended quite well among His Jewish brethren.

His hands were those you would expect of a carpenter and His sandals were well worn as though they had seen many places. Moving easily through the crowd, He was quite unassuming as He went about His business. Yet, there was no lagging. It was clear to see He was a man that knew what He was about and where He was going.

Following from a distance, I was soon taken by a gentleness

in His manner that bespoke His personality and character. Upon closer examination, I discovered there was something different, something different about His eyes . . . which were deep and eternal.

A certain presence drew me to Him. I wondered, is this the man they call the Son of God?

The Master's Touch

With eagerness I continued to follow Him. I was surprised when He stopped and stared. Shaded by aged stone buildings I, too, stopped and watched, curious at the deep concern imprinted upon His face.

Turning my head to see what could capture His attention so, I saw a widow and a funeral bier—her son lying upon it. Haggard, face drawn, shoulders sagging, her unfocused eyes enfolded her son. Her pain pulled at my heart. Colleagues in grief, compatriots in pain . . . her sorrow I knew all too well. Then I looked at the boy's hand. It had a ring similar to my own . . . what could it mean?

I was enthralled. I watched to see what this Man would

do. He seemed to be discerning and aware of all things. Even bustling city streets, with engulfing masses of humanity, could not distract Him from observing the widow's grief. Her only son dead, hopelessly alone and easily lost in the bedlam . . . she was not lost to the Master's view.

Drawn by her sorrow, it didn't take long for this Man to make up His mind. He moved forward with precise, deliberate movements and a firm but quiet resolution in His manner. Taller than the widow, He looked upon her. His eyes took hold of hers and gently He said, "Woman, weep not."

He stepped forward and commanded with firm and complete authority, "Young man, I say unto thee, arise."

The effect on the crowd was complete, as evidenced by widened eyes and stunned expressions. The spectators looked on with anxious anticipation which turned to shock and disbelief. First a twitch, then the boy's eyes fluttered, his hands moved, and . . . he sat upright on the bier.

I do not recall what the widow said, if indeed she said anything at all. I only remember what I felt as her arms consumed her returning son.

If this were the only event I witnessed, I would say, "Enough!" But, there's more . . . much, much more.

The Rejected

All were invited to come and partake. None were to escape the arms of His compassion, not even the man with the dreaded walking death. Rejected, scorned, labeled unclean, the sorrowful creature full of leprosy fell down at His feet as the crowd gave way. He pitifully pleaded, "Lord if thou wilt, thou canst make me clean."

Neither the sight of the decaying flesh nor the stifling odor could hinder His healing touch. Without hesitation, He stretched forth His hand saying, "I will. Be thou clean." Mere words would not suffice. The Master reached forth and . . . touched him! People gasped in horror around Him.

As I followed, the crowds grew in size, hungering to witness this strange new phenomenon. With them, they brought their blind, deaf, crippled, and sick. The crowd pressed continually upon Him, offering no respite. He who walked on troubled waters thought it more significant to cross crowded streets to reach the lame and infirm.

Coming upon a deformed, misshapen man, He stopped, gave him careful consideration, then uttered the comforting words, "Son, be of good cheer. Thy sins are forgiven thee."

Then he, too, arose.

Born King of kings and Lord of lords, it was clear: He found more pleasure in the company of the meek and lowly of heart. Though by trade a carpenter, it was evident that mankind was His business.

Once again the crowd gave way in respect to an aged, diseased woman who painstakingly made her way to Him. Timidly she touched his garment. He turned and took in her presence. His eyes enveloped her in kindness.

Smiling, He reached forward and softly said, "Daughter, be of good comfort; thy faith has made thee whole."

How does one describe the majesty of it all? The crippled

walk, the blind see, the deaf hear, and the dead live once again. But that is not all. Another healing took place. One much more difficult to describe . . . more profound and eternal. I saw it in the widow, the diseased woman, the leper, and many others . . . a look in their eyes, a change in their countenance, a smile on their faces.

Returning to the statue under the tree, I now understood the resilient smile on the girl's face. The two girls were in fact the same—one before, the other after the touch of the Master's hand.

The Crystal

The next package, third in number, was small, gentle blue, and light to the touch—the reflection of a fine autumn sky. A glimmering crystal teardrop drew my attention as it reflected the lights. Clear and pure, it gave tenfold of what it took in and offered many brilliant colors in return . . . much like the Good Shepherd who lighted the paths of others in many diverse ways. His wisdom and charity extended in all directions and to all people. His compassion, ever present, was most apparent one morning on a hill.

There was a bright, unrestricted sun that day, and shimmering rays reflected in the sparkling morning dew. Even in the early hours He was not alone. Long shadows followed the small crowd—a dozen and more—as they ascended a gently winding path.

Up He came, up and over the summit known as Olives. Once over the crest, He paused and took a long look at Jerusalem sprawling below. I watched Him search the ancient city, then gaze into the heavens beyond. It was a long, distant look . . . as though His eyes were taking in more than what my mortal eyes could see.

It was a kindly man I saw standing there, a man lost in His thoughts. Then, as though His thoughts had a will of their own, He sighed. It was an extended sigh. His words had a fatigued, forlorn feeling that touched my heart. "Oh, Jerusalem, Jerusalem—how often I would have gathered thee, even as hen gathereth her chicks, but ye would not."

Then, to my surprise . . . He wept.

I closely followed the journey of his tears. It seemed the earth reached up and affectionately took them onto herself. I watched the moisture christening the ground and thought, what divine tears these were, for soon the earth, too, would weep.

Lost in these thoughts, I was pulled back to the crystal

teardrop's elegance. Again I was enthralled by the brilliance of the colors that mystified my eyes. Moved by the tenderness of what I had just seen, I returned it to its shelter under the tree.

The Garden

My eyes moved to the fourth gift . . . a huge red package. I was struck by its enormity and wondered how it could be so massive. There was a certain loneliness about it, a loneliness shared by a miniature porcelain tree isolated in the corner, standing vigil, as though it were a witness . . . but a witness to what?

As my attention was absorbed by the ornament, I found myself standing by another tree—an ancient sentinel by the looks of its leathered-laced limbs.

A gentle breeze whispered as I surveyed the garden before me. Curious, I wondered where I was and why I was there. Upon close examination I knew! "This is the place," I whispered. This is where it happened!

The Eight Gift

Of all consecrated ground, this was the most holy because of what happened here. Of all events sanctifying hallowed ground, none was more electrifying, more transcending, more significant . . . than Gethsemane!

So engrossed was I that I did not notice the party entering the garden. It was a voice, His voice, that caused me to turn.

His words hung heavily and were as laden as His countenance. "Watch ye here with me, for my soul is filled with sorrow even unto death." A surprising declaration accentuated by slow, deliberate movements.

Leaving his companions behind, He moved forward in the darkness . . . alone, His usual quick and lengthy strides gone, replaced by slow, labored, almost dragging of His feet. His shoulders hung low as though they were weighed down by an oppressive mantle . . . a most ponderous weight.

The weight increased as He moved forward—heavier and heavier, bowing Him down more and more, bringing Him down to his knees. A groan escaped His lips. I could not discern all His words, but I did hear an imploring, beseeching prayer: "O Father, if it be possible, let this cup pass from me."

I was stunned! What pain could be so sore, so exquisite, so hard to bear that even Christ should shrink from its onslaught?

I looked upward and noted . . . this night of nights seemed darker than usual. The stars lost their luster. Even the moon abandoned us in the night.

A sudden stillness prevailed. The breeze died, replaced by a deathly quiet. The earth stopped. Time would not move onward. The night of ransom extracted its dues . . . the last farthing paid in complete fullness.

A hushed anxiety overcame me as well. Compelled, my eyes came back to His face. I was captivated. Though a chill ran through my bones, His forehead glistened. A trembling took place under His cloak. And something more, something I had never before seen and hope to never again witness: The anguish, the agony, was unspeakable. Words flee my pen, they fail me, they pale into nothing. The strain, so unrelenting, ever so great—his pores could not hold back! Staining his clothing were countless crimson droplets!

I marveled at this. How could this thing be? And why? Why, oh why?

The Eight Gift

I cannot describe the groaning I heard that night. I shudder at the remembrance of it.

It was then that something remarkable happened—something that should not have surprised me. The nobility of it simply over-whelmed me. Immortal words privileged my ears—words that encapsulated His soul . . . the essence of His character . . . in short, the complete epitaph of His life. So simply said, so eloquently spoken and infinitely noble: "Father, not my will, but thine, be done."

Why would He willingly submit to such an ordeal? What could motivate Him so? As I watched . . . I knew. What I had witnessed had captured the last full measure of my heart.

Suddenly He arose and approached His sleeping disciples saying, "Sleep and take your rest; the hour is at hand. The Son of Man is betrayed into the hands of sinners."

It was then I noticed the lights approaching. With purposeful intent they entered the garden. I surveyed their faces. I peered into their eyes . . . there was no mistaking the look therein.

The blazing torches were dull. They couldn't burn any hotter than the fire which raged in the hearts of those who this night would seek to destroy the Light of the World.

A man dressed in dark garb, darker than the night, came forward and hurriedly kissed Him on the cheek. Though he kissed Him, he would not look squarely at Him, as though the ground was the master of his eyes.

As swift as flashing swords, the ensuing events spun me in a daze. My thoughts ran many directions in confusion. Bewildered, I sat upon a rock, not knowing where to turn or where to go. I looked up, wanting to call out, but . . . He was gone.

I cannot measure what was in my heart. Time and space had lost all bearing . . . like falling . . . endlessly falling . . . in a darkened abyss. When I looked again, the garden was empty . . . as empty as my heart.

The dream moved onward.

Again I found myself by my friend . . . the Christmas tree. Seeking comfort in the gifts, I looked about. Two packages came to my attention. Though, they were different in color, they were twins in size, and were, in fact, a mirror reflection of the same gift, much like twins attached at birth, wanting to disjoin, but linked together forever . . . for one could not live without the other.

One was wrapped in black with silver edging, the other was

of shining gold, a card with bold print hanging loosely from it. My mind numb, almost shattered, I could not read the message thereon.

I addressed its brother—the black and silver package. My heart was not content to linger on the wooden emblem adorning its wrapping. Rather, my mind moved onward, wanting to see more, wanting to know more.

If my dream had experienced spring, summer, and fall, then surely I now found myself in the darkest of winters—though it was an April night that confounded me.

It was a tumultuous anxious crowd that filled my view. A restless anxiety filled the air. Some must have hungered, for there was no time for the morning meal. Some hungered mightily for something more. It was more than the evening air that chilled my bones. I followed the events from a distance.

How do I describe what I saw? How do I measure its impact? How do I describe His face or the look thereon? I was awed by His resignation . . . His willingness . . . His commitment.

Again I looked into His eyes. If my heart were measured, it would match the stripes and torn condition of his back. My cheeks, too, bore stains, though not crimson-red like His.

Richard J. Harding

I was caught in the midst of the moving tide. I followed them to the hill. It was a very long journey, though the distance was not far. If I could, I would describe the look upon His face as He laid Himself upon the timber and watched as the nail was positioned for the first blow. At once, I wanted to leave but was unable to move . . . the earth and I had found a common bond.

Strange!

Strange how silence can take hold of a crowd and stillness prevail over one and all. Even I found myself holding my breath. I do not know how many anxious moments passed. The heavens were spellbound. I watched motionless, the hushed crowd with me. The climactic scene unfolded.

Suddenly, my ears were victimized! A revolting noise called . . . demanding my attention. The scraping, scratching, grinding of timber and stone meeting face to face. The reviling noise quickened, an increasing tempo, then a tumultuous thud! Mother earth shuddered and shivered at the impact . . . or perhaps, it was only I.

I searched the heavens looking for the pilgrim's star, wondering where it had gone. Had we traveled so far for it all to be in vain?

The Eight Gift

Silhouetted against an angry sky, He looked down upon us, taking in His final view. Pain and fatigue His constant companions, still He spoke. His words revealed the supreme nobility of his character. Even then, His words were, "Father, forgive them!"

There were other nails driven that day. I felt them deep within my heart. I was powerless, speechless . . . I could only watch!

Despite the goodness of His heart and the tenderness of His soul, He . . . the greatest of all . . . died.

I will not dwell on the events of the next three days. Suffice it to say, mortal history has never recorded darker nights.

The Tomb

The sun was slow in making its appearance, and Mary's head hung low as she approached. She did not see it—the stone had been moved! With a shock it captured her attention! Her fingers caught her breath, her feet hastened, then . . . she stopped, motionless, hesitant, bewildered. Winning the fight, slowly, irresistibly drawn, she looked within, but all that met her eyes was a silent, empty chamber.

So taken was she that she did not see Him. Nor did she recognize the voice. "Woman, why weepest thou?"

Surprised, I turned, and my heart leapt! Though but a few paces away, the distance was impassable . . . I dared not intrude.

Supposing Him to be the gardener, Mary's reply was quick

and urgent, "Sir, if thou hast borne Him hence, tell me where thou hast laid Him and I will take Him away."

Her heart pierced, gloom her only companion, the blackness of a starless night was no darker than the veil in her eyes or the anguish in her voice. But darkness had its final hour!

Since that occasion, I have marveled at the power of a single word. The power to change all-consuming grief to joy and happiness.

Just one word . . . and what tenderness, what compassion, what gentle, loving regard filled that word. Jesus, looking upon this faithful woman, simply said, "Mary!"

With a gasp, a jerk, she looked up. Her eyes, her mouth, recoiling . . . then smiling. Her eyes afire, burning brightly. Her soul aglow, rejoicing. Her face alive, beaming, bursting. A new dawn had risen.

As cascading waters filled the soul and overflowed with brimming brine, my fingers sought the gold package under the familiar lights of the tree. The sleek surface, smooth to my tender touch, shimmered in soft reflection. My tears anointed the foil. Anxiously I looked more closely at the card hanging from it. The elation in Mary's voice, the lightness in her footsteps, all still vivid to my memory. I read her message.

"Come see, the tomb is empty. Come see, death is no longer. Come see, the Lord is risen. Christ lives . . . death is conquered. Life eternal is for the taking!"

Again I sat under the enveloping lights of the tree, amazed how, through death, came victory. Because of Him, our destinies are assured.

I measured the price of this golden gift . . . and found it priceless!

The Pearl

If these were all the gifts, in contentment my speech would fail me. But, lingering in the branches, was one other . . . the seventh gift.

It was a small box, almost tiny, with a snow-white pearl— the pearl adorning an elegant, creamy-white wrapping. My heart trembled. I shivered at the joy of it. Like many gifts, the smallest is often the most valuable.

It was a radiant day when next I saw Him sitting on the brow of a hill, His voice distinct, vibrant, and unwavering. There was a small crowd, only a few souls sitting about his feet.

His words created a warmth more radiant than the afternoon sun, and a swelling within, broader than the azure sky behind him. He spoke with an affluent easiness and a smile that brought a quietness to my soul. He spoke of glorious events and eternal promises; of going to His Father and of preparing a place; of not fearing and of having a constant companion.

Then my heart stopped . . . my breath escaped me . . . our eyes met! In that one riveting moment, those eyes spoke to me! They spoke of friendship, love, and that we would meet again. They spoke of exalted themes and remarkable possibilities.

Seven gifts He has given to me . . . and to all. I cannot say which I appreciate the most; but to know His friendship . . . His love . . . and that I am never alone, brings a peace that surpasses all understanding.

Truly, I too, stand all amazed. While the earth received a King . . . I found a friend!

The Noble Birthright

I sat under the warmth of the tree, overwhelmed at the seven gifts that lay before me. As their significance touched my senses, I was filled with understanding.

Because angels sang, we sing. Because Christ gave, we give. Christmas is more than a carousel of activities . . . more than a holiday . . . it is a noble birthright. Christmas is a celebration of life itself. Christmas enshrines all the noblest virtues of mankind . . . and joyful are they who discover and revel in its treasures.

As I contemplated the magic wand, and this great invisible blanket that gently rests upon us each season, I ponder the impact of these gifts and the effect they have upon us. For if they embody the spirit of this Man, the One they call Christ, then surely this Spirit, the Spirit of Christ, is also a noble birthright and, in the end, may be the greatest gift of all.

The Harbor

The warmth of the dream was all-pervading. It was peaceful, reassuring . . . like being snugly enfolded in a thick feather comforter, right up to the neck on a frost-bitten night. Supremely, my spirit smiled. Yet, upon further reflection, the candid truth, like a pointed barb, proclaimed, I was full, but not complete. Something was missing.

A choir can sing, a concert can play, and symphony songs can fill the heavens, but with empty notes and dull refrain if the heart cannot sing or be with those who make it sing the loudest!

It was a bitter battle that bewitched my soul, an all-consuming battle. I will not belabor the details nor the event that altered my life. I shall simply say, on a cold, wintry night, they left—or should I say were taken?—leaving a void . . . a pain . . . an indescribable ache within. A wife, a son, a daughter, three angels to my memory.

My son, young and slender, his head would meet my chin. My daughter, a wee little lass with cheerful laugh, had dimpled cheeks and curly little locks.

Of my wife I have much to say. It is all written within my heart. A harbor of memories . . . moonlight walks and midnight talks; sharing a child's first cry and coaching his newly made footsteps; little quarrels with heartfelt apologies; weekend trips and private enclosures; perfumed hair and playful, slender fingers.

A harbor of memories . . . reminding me that the substance, merit, meat of life is found in those gems which give it the most flavor.

If I had but one wish, it would be to feel their cheeks, cheek to cheek, and touch their hearts, heart to heart. If I had but one wish. . . .

The Eighth Gift

Frozen, motionless, in a silent sinewed stupor, I sat. A minute, no, a lifetime passed. Transfixed in my thoughts, I did not, at first, see the new light. Slowly, consistently, with each new beat of my heart, it grew brighter and brighter until it filled the room brilliantly.

Looking to its source, at first I thought it to be a star crowning the pinnacle of the tree. But, as the diamond-shaped luster lured me into its sanctum, I saw it for what it was. My eyes narrowed tightly—focusing . . . I recognized the token!

I thought it strange that something so small and round should hold such a place of honor. I was puzzled at its significance. Then as night and light merged at dawn, my mind awakened. I understood the whole of it. It was the star, the pilgrim's star, that called my name; and what was once the pilgrim's star was now the sage's scepter.

The birth was the beginning, the resurrection promised new life, and the atonement gives passage. His compassionate invitation still lingers, and His healing touch binds the wounds of mortality. His friendship became a lasting personal gift, yet symbolic of all lasting relationships and the enduring quality of perpetual ties and bonds we treasure most.

If it was the star that called my name, it was the ring that was the signet that sealed the love, encompassed the message, and enfolded the promises. The ring encircled it all, symbolizing exchanged vows and cherished promises and the power to give the vows everlasting meaning. Now I know . . . a circle is complete and never ends.

I looked at the ring. I thought of my wife, my children. I was hopeful, but uncertain . . . how could I be sure? I found doubt to be a devious demon.

In the midst of all these thoughts, it happened. I felt a breeze, a blissful breeze . . . I turned.

As tall timbers and towering pines dance to a mighty wind . . . so my senses reeled. No ocean could sway or swoon with stronger tide, and no Easter sunrise could shine the brighter.

Her hair, her dress . . . like flowing satin . . . her radiance, filled my vision. Her eyes, the bluest eyes, glistened . . . diamonds kissed by a morning mist. She spoke no words; she had no need, her face said it all. She stretched forth her hand.

If I could have a single, last embrace—and who's to say I didn't?—can you imagine what final words my arms would impress upon her?

Yes, it is sacred soil within my breast, and there is little more to say, except I knew, and knew it well . . . I fully understood. It's the melodies of the heart which are everlasting, and it's a happy home and hearth that understands: relationships live forever and are one's greatest treasure. It is the melodies of the heart that give it value.

When all was said and done, she reached out, placed it in my hand, then left. My throat tightened; my eyes froze; my neck, my limbs, were cast of stone, my fist clenched tightly about it. A choke, a sob, and I awoke.

The Eight Gift

Was it merely a dream? Maybe. Was it simply a figment of my imagination? Perhaps. However, there is more you must know.

Before I proceed, I must ask: was I truly awake or was I slumbering and sleeping still? It matters not, for the story ends the same . . . and succinct, sublime serenity stills my soul.

The morning rays lit more than the panes of my window as I lay upon my bed. A single beam, sure and true, framed and lit my fist with a lustrous glow.

I thought of the Man upon the hill. I recalled His words.

I remembered my wife . . . and her flowing satin.

HIS words . . . HER hair.

HIS eyes . . . HER smile.

I looked upon my fist . . . I wondered . . .

Could it be?

Was it possible?

Slowly, my fingers relaxed, opening like the petals of a spring flower.

There, sitting, shining, singing to my heart . . . the token of our love . . .

MY WIFE'S MATCHING RING!

About the Author

Richard Harding's life was altered dramatically while serving as a Marine in Vietnam during the Tet Offensive in 1968. The lessons he learned, the valiance he witnessed, and the respect he holds for Marines and veterans, then and now, have molded his life with profound appreciation and a desire to give something more.

The *Eighth Gift* is a pilgrimage of sorts . . . inviting the reader into a journey of discovery much like he has experienced through his life.

www.ingramcontent.com/pod-product-compliance
Lightning Source LLC
Chambersburg PA
CBHW060537030426
42337CB00021B/4303